Antreina E. Stone

POLE-DATE
Or
SOUL-MATE

Man In Blue
Esther's Story
Volume 2

Get More In Life Coaching, LLC
West Bloomfield, Michigan 48322

Paperback edition printed in the United States in 2017 by Get More in Life Coaching, LLC Text Copyright © Antreina E. Stone 2017

Although every precaution has been taken in the preparation of this book, the publisher and author assume no responsibility for errors or omissions. Neither is any liability assumed for damages resulting from the use of this information contained herein.

The right of Antreina E. Stone to be identified as the Author of the Work has been asserted by the Copyright, Designs and Patents Act 1988.

All rights reserved. No part of this publication may be reproduced, stored in a retrieval system, or transmitted in any form or by any means, electronic, mechanical, photocopying, recording or otherwise, without the prior written permission of the publisher.

Printed in the United States

Pole-Date Or Soul-Mate: Man In Blue Esther's Story

Antreina E. Stone

Edited:

Cary Morton https://authorunpublished.wordpress.com/

SBN-10: 0-9896975-4-1

ISBN-13: 978-0-9896975-4-5

10 9 8 7 6 5 4 3 2

About the Book

Pole-Date Or Soul-Mate: Man in Blue Esther's Story

Volume 2

Esther happens to bump into an old High School friend, becomes distracted, and ends up where no one wants to go, but many have. Vashti finds herself in need of support and seeks Paul, who is nowhere to be found. Meanwhile, Elizabeth and Vashti meet unexpectedly and Valerie shares a story with Esther that stops her in her tracks. Here comes the man in blue, driving a red Mustang and causing the heat to rise in *Pole-Date or Soul-Mate: Man In Blue Esther's Story Volume 2*

The story continues from volume 1, the journey of Esther being Single and Dating after an Unexpected Divorce.

Volume 1 Headline Reviews

"A must read for all single and married women"
Nadine Coleman

"The book is phenomenal"
Carolyn Henderson

"Great Read"
Joi Bodiford-Grear

"I read the book in one day and really enjoyed the characters"
  Wanda Bush

"Truly an eye opener"
Cynthia Wood

"Blessings in a book"
Kim Padgett

Dedication

Thank you to my fans who have supported my journey as an author, to my family and friends who continue to pray for me, and the most important one of all, God, who continually nurtures me to grow in the Power of His words. Purposely and productively, I continue to write with your encouragement and support. And as always, to my husband Willie Louis Stone and Antreina's Earrings Supporters, Love you!

Author Antreina E. Stone

Home Sweet Home

Silence lingered throughout the five-hour flight from Venezuela to LaGuardia Airport in New York. As the plane taxied toward the gate, Esther tapped her foot in anticipation as she waited to exit the aircraft. Valerie and Esther glanced at each other with matching smirks on their faces and shook their heads. Esther spoke first.

"Welcome to America, the land of the brave."

"We are two brave women that have traveled from far away and returned safely—albeit nothing gained," Valerie replied.

Valerie and Esther exchanged numbers after they had retrieved their luggage. They both lived outside of New York, across the George Washington Bridge in Jersey City. Although headed in the same direction, they'd already had enough of each other on the long trip and decided to go their separate ways. Valerie arranged for an Uber and Esther hopped into a Yellow Cab Taxi.

After giving the taxi driver her destination, there were twenty minutes of silence before the taxi driver spoke up.

"So, where are you from? I don't mean to pry, but it's been a busy day and you're my last passenger for the night."

"Why do you ask? It's your job to take me to my destination, not ask questions." After a deep breath, she replied in a softer voice, "Venezuela."

The cab driver pretended as though he hadn't heard her earlier response. He seemed to understand that she'd had a long day. "Was there a women's convention or something over there?"

"No, why do you ask?"

"You're the fifth lady returning from Venezuela in my cab today! I find it very interesting, that's all. It just came in over the radio that another one from Venezuela just called in."

"Oh, really? I can only imagine. I hope their trip was a hundred times better than mine." Esther rolled her eyes as she stared out the passenger window on the opposite side of the cab.

The cab driver frequently checked the rear view mirror as they approached their destination. He stared at Esther through his mirror as she fumbled through her mega purse, searching for her wallet. She frantically tossed things from her purse onto the back seat of the cab, eager to pay him. The cab driver waited politely and removed her luggage as he waited for her to exit the cab.

Finally, Esther paid the taxi fare. "Thank you." Her voice was weak, worn down by the experience of her time in Venezuela. She gravely moved toward her porch, where a thick stack of mail spilled out of her mailbox. She attempted to grab her mail despite both hands being full; which caused a handful of letters to fall onto the porch. The cab driver dashed to rescue her in the overwhelming moment as Esther fumbled with her hands and arms full. For a moment, he'd startled Esther; she hadn't noticed the driver was still sitting in front of her home. Esther sat her luggage inside her door and the Taxi driver handed her the pieces of dropped mail he'd collected.

"Goodnight." He said as he turned to leave.

Before he'd stepped off the porch, Esther stopped him. "Since this is your last stop, do you want to come in and have a cup of coffee? I'd appreciate the company."

The cab driver studied her for a moment but nodded. To Esther, he seemed compassionate. "Sure, I don't mind."

A few minutes later, Esther handed him a freshly brewed cup of coffee. "I know this is an awkward situation. Would you like cream or sugar? Are you married?"

"Light cream, no sugar, please. Divorced; 3 years. My ex-wife slept with my brother and my father after I slept with her sister. She wanted to retaliate. I wasn't hurt by her, not really. My pain comes from my father and brother—they betrayed my trust. They knew she was my wife, and they could have—*should have*—walked away."

Esther sat in silence, taking deep breaths, reflecting back on her experience in Venezuela as she listened to the cab driver.

"But couldn't the same be said for you? You knew they were sisters. What makes that any less painful for your ex-wife? Pardon my asking." She looked at the cup of coffee in her hands. "I'm glad I invited you for coffee, but it seems you needed to talk more than me."

The hour was approaching midnight. Esther was exhausted from the two days she'd sat at the Airport and the long flight home, and she still hadn't showered.

"It's okay. You're right, and I understand why you asked. Anyways, it's getting late. I must leave."

"I'll share my experience the next time."

He paused and then nodded. "Sure." The taxi driver handed Esther his business card. "My name's James, by the way. Thank you for the coffee."

"Esther." She replied. "It was nice talking to you, James."

She thought it was strange that he hadn't answered her questions as she locked her door behind James. Though she really couldn't blame him for avoiding them, it was obviously a touchy subject.

Prepared for Bed

She tried to push the questions out of her head as she took a shower and prepared for bed.

Early the next morning, Esther still wanted to talk to someone, since James had taken up most of the time they'd shared telling his own story. She called her nature trail buddies, eager to walk and talk to clear her mind, but before Esther had even started dialing, Elizabeth called Esther instead.

Elizabeth explained that she'd been thinking of her and wanted to know how things were going. Since Esther had returned from her trip, Elizabeth invited her to meet-up on the nature trail. Esther agreed, immediately thinking to invite Valerie. She let Elizabeth know she was going to invite another lady to come along, and Elizabeth replied that she'd meet them on the trail.

Esther had good intentions in asking Valerie on the nature trail, but she wondered if it was the best idea at the moment. She followed her instincts and called Valerie anyhow.

Esther asked Valerie if she wanted to go for a walk and clear her head with some ladies who were willing to listen and talk about their experiences as well as sharing their own. Valerie was surprised that Esther had called as it hadn't been a full twenty-four hours since they had returned home, but she agreed to meet up at Vashti's Boutique as it was close to her work.

The Meet Up

Surprisingly when Esther arrived, she noticed Valerie sitting on the bench, and nearby stood Elizabeth and Rachel. She greeted Elizabeth and Rachel and they hugged as Valerie waited nearby. The three women walked towards Valerie as Esther beckoned her to come over. The ladies welcomed Valerie with a brief introduction and a smile, already knowing that if she had been invited to join them, there had to be a relationship problem involved. Naturally, because of their younger age, Valerie and Rachel connected, leaving Elizabeth and Esther to walk together.

Elizabeth asked Esther as they began walking to tell her about the trip to Venezuela. Esther paused because the story wasn't only about her, but Valerie as well. She stepped to the side of the path while Valerie and Rachel continued walking. They hadn't yet noticed that Esther and Elizabeth had stopped. Esther struggled to think of the best way to explain their embarrassing experience.

"Esther, you zoned out on me. Did you hear me? I asked, 'how was your trip'?" Elizabeth prodded.

"Yeah, I heard you. I'm just not sure how best to tell you about it," she replied.

Esther took a deep breath. "I was made to look like a fool… and what's even better is that I found another fool beside me. We'd taken the same flight with the intention to visit the same man. It made me feel a little less awful— Esther chuckled. —knowing I wasn't the only one to fall for his lies. I ignored the little voice in my head telling me to back away from the very beginning and went anyway, and I ended up back where I started." She chuckled again, shaking her head.

Elizabeth raised her eyebrows in surprise and then slowly joined Esther, laughing even louder than her. "Wow! I knew something led me to tell you about Paul. I suppose the other fool was me."

"Oh no! At least you married him." She laughed, then took a deep breath. "I meant Valerie. We met with the same agenda in mind. The big difference between us is that she'd been traveling regularly to meet him and this was only my first time. I make it sound like I'm a virgin." She smiled. "But trust me, I'm not."

"No! Valerie? Oh, Esther!" She grabbed Esther, pulling her into a tight hug.

By this time, Valerie and Rachel had stopped walking and stood nearby, waiting for Esther and Elizabeth to catch up with them.

They stood together in a circle. Valerie looked at Esther and felt as if she'd shared their disappointing trip. She was very grateful Esther invited her along, realizing how important it was for her to be around the other women, who'd also experienced bad relationships and needed to get it off their chest. Everyone there had felt pain, and in her book, pain was pain.

"Esther, sometimes things happen in unpredictable ways. I'm so glad to join you ladies. Your support means so much to me. I don't feel the same as when I left home. I shared our story with Rachel and found she'd overcame far more than I've experienced. Walking it off and talking about it has helped, and I think in the future if we think about our mistakes and pray, things will change." Valerie smiled at the other women.

"Amen!" They unanimously agreed.

"Valerie, what an awesome way to put it. Leave your worries behind. Yes! I'm certain that if I hadn't gone to get my pictures back, you could have very well been saying your forever afters to an imposter. Perhaps it was God's will that we met." Esther reached out and squeezed her hand in solidarity.

"What pictures?" The other women asked.

"Well, let's just say that they were worth traveling to another country to retrieve." She hoped that said enough. That very moment Esther froze, as she couldn't recall seeing the SD card with her pictures once she'd gotten home. She'd merely forgotten about it. She began to question herself--was she sure they were safe at home?

"I bet I know what happened. Did you use Skype?" Rachel asked.

"Yes!"

"Well, did you record it?" Elizabeth laughed "You know you could have. I've recorded and sold copies." She looked around at the shocked faces of the other women. "What? I wasn't born on Mars. I told you, I screw em and leave them. In those exact words and order."

"Honey, is it because Paul left and you felt screwed? You must let it go!" Esther commented.

"I know this is my first time on the walk, and not to make any assumptions, but aren't the steps on the path meant to open and clear the way?As they say, 'Walk It, Talk It and Leave It' and of course, if you think about it, pray? You'll never get to the finish line if you respond with the same pain that's been visited upon you-- that's begging to be healed deep within you. You're hurting yourself all over again. Instead of using a band-aid, I hope you're using condoms at the very least," Valerie added.

Elizabeth spoke up. "Let me just say something, young lady. Weren't you saved from being miserable? I wasn't as lucky as you. You were stopped by this woman—" She pointed to Esther, "--who wanted to retrieve her naked pictures. She just so happened to book the same flight as yours. Lucky you! You both saved each other. We aren't all as fortunate. I traveled the thousands of miles, gave my word, and said I do. For what? He sweet talked my bank account dry. I was blind for 15 years, blind to the truth." Her eyes filled with tears. "It has been almost two years, and no… I haven't seen or heard from him."

"Elizabeth, I'm sorry, but didn't you say it has been two years?" Valerie asked. "You sound like those women who say they are still carrying baby weight from their pregnancy, and when you ask how long it's been, they say three years! You can't keep torturing yourself; you must let go. The more you lay with men to get back at your husband, the more pain and agony you're going to cause for yourself. You really need to look at the more positive things in life, like the better days that lie ahead, or the very moment we're sharing now. You're strong, beautiful, capable, and able to turn your life around and away from a pole-date. Trying to get back at your husband by doing what he did to you isn't going to hurt him, it's only going to hurt you," she cautioned.

"There's no greater sin against the body than sexual immortality." She continued. "Get it together! Forget about Paul. He's out of your life, and you should be glad about that. It had nothing to do with you, and it has nothing to do with the men you're sleeping with. Paul made that choice for himself because that was all he was thinking about—himself. You're doing yourself a disservice by giving yourself away to so many unworthy men. At least give yourself the benefit of the doubt, you deserve better, but you'll never see it until you let go of the anger you have towards Paul."

"Wow, Valerie, you're quite wise for someone so young. You talk as though you've been married twenty times." Esther said, and everyone chuckled.

"Can you imagine as a young child sitting in bed while your mom is in the next room getting her brains screwed out? From the age of seven, I watched my mom in and out of bed with different men, until finally, I was old enough to leave. I used to lock my bedroom door and keep my younger siblings in the room with me. I didn't show my face or make a sound. I don't think my mom even knew we were there. I'd listen to the moaning and groaning throughout the night and I would pray to God. I told Him that I didn't want to be like my mother. I watched disgusting men parade around our home in their undies with no regard for me or my siblings—all five of us. We all have different fathers, you know? My dad was the only one who bothered to put food on the table. When he left, he not only left my mom, he also left me—he never returned," Valerie explained.

She glanced around the group before continuing. "I know how it feels to have siblings with different fathers. I saw the hurt in their eyes when my dad and I interacted. They didn't have a relationship with their fathers, and it caused animosity between us. Their fathers never saw their pain because they valued a cheap feel over protection. Even though my father tried to give them as much attention as he possibly could, no man can fill the void of spending time with your own father."

"I understand your concern, and I appreciate it, Elizabeth ... but I'm not out screwing and sitting on top of every pole that comes my way. Am I angry? Yah, sometimes I am. Do I think about it, yes—but when I do, I pray!"

Everyone stood in the circle in awe for a few moments before coming closer together and engaging in a group hug. "Walk it. Talk it. Leave it. Pray." They all repeated the words together.

"Wow, what an excellent time together. You know, I was feeling ashamed of being single and turning fifty, and I hadn't even taken the time to celebrate my birthday!" Esther said. "My friend Vashti once said to me, 'It's never too late to celebrate you.' And you know what? I feel like it's time for a celebration!" She smiled at the other women. "Anyone up for cocktails? Are you ladies ready to *evolve*?"

A unanimous cheer went through the group as they all agreed with Esther's idea. They were surprised that Esther had not celebrated her birthday but also understood why. As they turned to leave, Esther asked for a couple of days to find a nice venue to meet up for cocktails. Everyone's burdens seemed lighter, especially Esther's. She felt free. She got into her car and cruised away, smiling as she waved goodbye to the other ladies.

Esther's attention was drawn to the complex where Vashti's Boutique use to be. A Starbucks sat a few doors down in the complex that she hadn't noticed before. The thought of an iced coffee made her mouth water, and she turned into the complex. As she entered Starbucks, she found the line was all the way to the door. Customers stood in the queue, talking about the George Washington Bridge as it had been closed for hours going into New York.

There had been an accident.

Esther had planned to drive over to Manhattan to shop for a party dress for her birthday celebration. She knew there were more boutiques there than in her area, and she had not wanted to spend thousands of dollars as she'd done at Vashti's Boutique and Sak's Fifth Avenue. Finally, the barista called Esther's name for her iced latte, and she grabbed it before exiting the coffee shop.

Esther was only a few miles away from home, and instead of rushing to get there, she decided to sit at a nearby table and take in the scenery. It was a beautiful day outside—though there wasn't much to look at other than the birds in the air, a few blooming flowers, and people going in and out of Starbucks. The table's location gave her a clear view to the main street that led to the bridge. As she settled into her seat, she noticed a tow truck that was hauling the crumpled remains of a yellow vehicle. Her chair screeched as she stood up abruptly, knocking over her coffee in front of her. When she'd heard the people in the coffee shop talking about an accident, she'd never imagined it'd be someone she knew. She grabbed her forehead in disbelief.

Oh my gosh, I hope Vashti's okay!

The yellow sports car was easily recognizable. Esther had never seen one like it and she'd never forget it's distinct color.

Esther immediately dialed Vashti's number, but there was no answer.

She didn't have anyone else's number other than Valerie's, so that is who she called.

"Esther, did you hear? Vashti was in an accident and had to be airlifted by helicopter off the George Washington Bridge!" Valerie rushed through the words on the other end of the line even before Esther had finished saying hello.

"No!" She exclaimed. "I can't believe this is happening—that's why I was calling you. I just saw a tow truck drive by with a yellow sports car on the bed, and I just knew it was hers." She stared aghast at the busy street, the tow truck now out of sight. She was numb with shock and couldn't even shed a tear.

"Shh Esther, it'll be all right." Valerie comforted her as she watched her TV in the background where a news report talked about the accident. She listened for the name of the hospital Vashti would be taken to.

They both held the phone for several minutes in silence.

Upon hanging up, Esther left the complex, leaving the mess of her coffee behind. She didn't have time to worry about that now, needed to know more. Was Vashti okay?

Her phone rang. It was Valerie.

"What did you find out?" She gnawed on her lip as she waited in anticipation for Valerie's response.

"She was taken to a hospital nearby in Jersey City."

"Would you like to go with me?"

"Esther, I would love to, but…"

"But what?"

"I'm not sure she'll want to see me."

"Hell, we don't even know if she's alive! Come with me and let's find out. It's time to put the BS behind us and move forward. You act like you slept with her man or something."

"Esther, I have."

Esther paused, half-way in her car, one foot still on the pavement. Did she want to know? Was it even her business? She took a deep breath. *Lord, how am I going to get through this?* Before she could ask Valerie to repeat herself, her friend blurted out the story.

"Esther, that's why I stop working for Vashti. I use to stay late at night and John would always come by to make sure the store was locked. Well, one evening I couldn't help myself. He was dressed in a white button-down collared shirt, he smelled good, and you already know he's muscular and handsome. The lights were low while I was in the back clearing out a fitting room, and he stretched his arms over the doorway and blocked me from passing through. It happened so fast, all of it. Vashti always appeared to be happy, and I'll admit, I wanted some of her happiness. She talked constantly about John, how good he was to her, the things he'd done for her and the places they were planning to go. I didn't have that. After that, John and I would meet regularly at the Boutique. He would always find out from Vashti when I would work late. I betrayed her.

"How could you betray Vashti like that? You knew they were involved. How long did this go on?" Esther had so many questions, even though none of them were really important right now.

"During the entire time, he was with Vashti, up until he was diagnosed with cancer. We met a few times after his treatments were done, but it wasn't the same. He couldn't hold an erection because of all the medication they'd had him on—but I knew before then that there wasn't going to be a future for us. I guess you can say, I share a lot more of my mom's DNA than I thought I did." There was a pause on the other end of the line as Valerie took a deep breath. "I regret it. I only wanted the life she was living. It seemed like all she talked about was John. John. John! I wanted what she had." She let out a laugh, but it had no humor in it.

"Hell, I even attended John's bachelor party. Did you know that? He had four of his closest friends there that night. It was during a time when I needed money and I was only working part time for Vashti—but instead of collecting a paycheck, I had fun with John and his friends. He asked me to join him and his friends for a night of fun. It was something I'd always wanted to do, at least once." Her voice sounded tired, and Esther listened quietly to her story.

"I didn't think of the outcome."

She paused. "They took turns, one by one. One of John's friends was really rough. I had bruises on my back and neck and a bite mark on my stomach." Her voice shook on the other end of the line as she began to weep. "John heard me screaming and came to my rescue. The guy had bitten me so hard it broke the skin and I screamed."

"Oh, Valerie..." Esther didn't know what to say. She could only imagine how frightened her friend must have been. Whatever choices Valerie had made, she didn't deserve what had happened to her. Surely she must have been so frightened.

"John was curious. I can still hear him shouting 'What the hell is wrong with you?'. He asked his friend to leave, and he was very apologetic. He kept saying over, and over how sorry he was, but I just laid there, feeling worthless." She sniffled.

"Do you know what he said as he was leaving? He said I was nothing but another whore waiting to be screwed. He branded me with his 'bi**h bite' so that every time I saw it I'd be reminded of it... and I have been. Every day."

"Valerie, what happened wasn't your fault. Maybe your choices weren't right, but that doesn't give that man the right to harm you. He made that choice. You didn't ask him to do it or give him permission. What he did, doesn't make you… *less.*"

"Maybe, but I can't face Vashti, and I'm sure I'd be the last person she wants to wake up and see."

Esther was aghast at what had happened to Valerie. Her stomach turned and eyes watered as she listened and felt Valerie's pain. She'd carried this burden for so long.

"One evening, after John's cancer treatment, Vashti caught us at the boutique. I can still see her face and hear the sound of her voice as she realized we'd betrayed her. She left John, fired me, and closed the dress boutique. Shortly afterward, I started the online relationship with Ralph. He caught me at a vulnerable moment." Valerie explained.

Esther held the phone in silence. Rather than questioning Valerie any further, she needed to comfort her. "Look, Valerie. We have a lot in common. We were both tricked by these men, and we both made mistakes we wish we could take back, but now isn't the time to cry over spilled milk. Vashti needs our support, and we need to set our differences aside and move forward. Please, meet me at the hospital."

Esther understood how it felt to want to belong and get along with someone. Especially, the one you loved. Her memory danced back to her and Daniel, recalling a time in their marriage when she'd agreed to an open marriage. She would've done anything to keep her husband. He'd wanted more from her, he wanted twice what she'd been able to give to him. Daniel was the kind of man who could talk you right out of your skin. She didn't understand what more he wanted from her, not until Daniel asked her to accompany him and another woman in bed.

He wanted to have a threesome.

It was tough for her to watch her husband and another woman go at it, lusting after one another. When Esther's turn came to join them, he would always get rough as he penetrated her. The deeper he penetrated, the harder the slaps. From the corner of her eyes, she'd seen the other woman's concern.

As Daniel's grunts grew louder than the slaps as he came, Esther recalled reaching out and grabbing his hand. He hadn't had enough strength left to restrain her. She'd forced him over onto his side, and then she slipped away to the bathroom. She'd locked the door as she wept. She recalled looking into the mirror at the hand marks left from Daniel's aggression.

She could imagine how Valerie felt every time she looked at the bite mark left on her body. How painful and disgusting it must have felt. She hoped Valerie had gotten a tetanus shot, or better yet, she should have that man arrested!

Esther struggled with how long she piecemealed her marriage together and was glad as hell to be out of that mud hole. She shouldn't have tried so hard to prolong what obviously wasn't working.

What had she been thinking?

Now that she was out, she could do whatever she wanted. The threesome should have been her first sign to run, but she'd chosen to stay in her marriage instead.

The Hospital

Esther was unsure if Valerie was going to meet her at the hospital. She understood Valerie's hesitation.

When she reached the patient information center she was surprised to find Valerie, who greeted her with a big hug and thanked her for listening earlier. Esther was the only person she'd shared her experience with.

Vashti was in the ICU. Only one visitor was allowed at a time. The curtains were drawn, and the doctors were in and out of the room. Esther and Valerie were told to wait awhile before they were allowed to go see Vashti. They'd been warned that she was bruised up pretty bad and going in and out of consciousness. She'd repeatedly asked for Paul.

The ICU nurse asked the women if either of them knew Paul, but Esther and Valerie both replied that they hadn't. She'd gone on to ask if Vashti had any relatives nearby, but if she did, neither women knew of them.

Esther went in to see Vashti first. Although the nurse had forewarned her, she was still surprised by Vashti's appearance. The person laying before her didn't look anything like the beautiful, perpetually dolled-up Vashti, whose walk turned heads. Machines beeped and wooshed, maintaining the steady rhythm of Vashti's life. Blue and green bruises shadowed her face. Her eyes were swollen shut, her head bandaged, and her neck was supported by a brace. She even had a small cast repairing the damage to her nose.

Oh my God!

Her hand hovered over her mouth in alarm.

"Oh, Vashti!" Would she be okay? *God, why did this happen to her?* Esther left the room, she couldn't help Vashti right now, and it was hard to see her friend so damaged.

On the way out she heard a weak voice whisper, *Paul.*

"Where the HELL IS Paul?" Esther demanded, nearly screaming as she left Vashti's room and headed for the nurse's station.

The nurse told Valerie and Esther that they were the only visitors Vashti had had since she'd come in. Esther wanted to know more about her condition, but the nurse could only give specifics to her closest relatives. The closest relative Esther and Valerie could think of was John, and he was now her ex-husband. Neither were sure if that would qualify.

"Valerie, do you still have John's number?" Esther turned towards her as she spoke.

"Yes, but *I'm* not calling him." She dug her phone out of her purse, holding it out.

"Now is not the time for that. Give it to me, I'll do it!" She took the phone and turned away from Valerie as she scrolled through her contacts, shaking her head at Valerie's stubborness.

"He's not next of kin."

"Who made you the executor of the estate? That's for the hospital to figure out, not you! Right now, we're the only people she's got, and if this is the only way we're going to get any information out of her nurse, then this is what we're going to do."

She finally found John's number. When Esther called, someone else answered and said that John was in Hospice, not doing well. Esther nearly dropped the phone, and slumped down into a nearby chair. As she gathered her thoughts, she asked the person on the line if John was going to be okay. She learned that John was in his final stage of passing, and the person on the phone wasn't sure if he'd make it till morning. The person on the other end asked who was calling, and Esther gave them her name before thanking them, and ending the call.

She felt terrible. She wished she hadn't called. John was dying and Vashti was in poor condition—and where was Paul?

Before leaving the hospital, Esther asked the nurse if she would call her when Vashti wasn't so sedated. She said she'd call from time to time to check in on her, but until Vashti was more coherant, she knew she'd learn little of her condition.

Esther and Valerie went their separate ways. Valerie asked when the next nature walk would be, but Esther wasn't sure. She told her she'd let her know. She'd need to check with Elizabeth.

Everything seemed to be so complicated at that moment. Esther couldn't put her life on hold because someone else's had taken a detour. She'd been there once--*not again!* The best she could do was pray for her friends. She asked God to give her understanding.

The A Train

She soon headed over to New York on the A Train. She still needed to shop for her party dress, and it would be a good distraction from the day's events. She was ready to evolve—and she had a birthday to celebrate.

The train was filled to capacity. Esther was able to squeeze into a nearby seat that no one else seemed to want to occupy. After sitting, she understood why. The person she sat next to reeked of alcohol and other unidentifiable odors. It didn't bother her, she hoped the fumes would work as a proxy for an actual drink. Esther had to admit, the thought was disgusting, even if it was true. She peeked from the corner of her eye at the man and found him looking at her as well. He was unkempt, though his shoes didn't look worn. The coat he wore seem to be made of good fabric. He really only needed to shave and shower.

"Hello." Esther greeted him.

He didn't say a word.

Esther said a silent prayer for the man.

God, please help this person I'm sitting next to. He's obvious going through something that only you can heal him from. After you deliver him, also deliver me, Valerie, Elizabeth, Rachel and in the name of Jesus. Thank you for healing Vashti and delivering Paul, Amen.

When you can't do anything else, pray!

After Esther silently prayed, the man sitting next to her finally spoke up. "Thank you for your prayers."

Esther jumped at his unexpected words. She turned to him. "How did you know I was praying?"

The man smiled. "God informed me there would be a seat no one else would take except the one person I'd give it to, and that they would pray for me, and I would be healed from my depression. He also told me that she would become my wife."

Esther, sat back in silence, her posture stiff. She didn't know what to say. She couldn't rebuke what he said. It was as though her mouth had been sealed. Ironically, the man she prayed for shortly exited at the next stop as she stared after him. She watched as he left the train several stops before hers.

WoMen On Notice Boutique

As Esther maneuvered her way through the crowded streets of Manhattan, she found herself walking as though they were empty. She felt the bumps as people passed her by, but her mind was too busy to acknowledge them. She found herself looking through a storefront window, at a funky dress that practically shouted, *It's your Birthday! Red! Fire! Hot!*

She entered the store and a full shapely woman inside reminded her of a friend of hers from North Carolina, Velma, that she hadn't seen since High School. She was flanked by two other women as they thumbed through a clothing rack. Esther waited to inquire about the dress, but the familiar woman called Esther's name.

"Esther, is that you?"

Esther was exhausted and she didn't respond right away.

A woman standing next to Velma spoke snidely to her friend. "I don't think she wants to be bothered. Some people think they're better than you until they find out who you are!"

Esther stood in silence, thinking; not right now, and not then. Esther turned. She ignored the rude woman who was with her friend. "Velma! Is that you? Wow!"

"Yes! I've gained a few curves. You know, sometimes bigger *is* better."

"I thought that was you! I just—"

"Oh, my weight!" She reached into her purse and handed Esther her business card that read:

Boobs + Waist + Hips = Plus Size!

Esther couldn't help but laugh. "Are you serious? That's awesome! I get it; embrace every inch of your body, right? Wow! You look good." She smiled. "So, are you still living in North Carolina?"

"Honey, I can be anywhere I want to be at anytime I want to be there. I—" She paused and gestured to her rude friend. "We actually fly in and shop, and to attend women conferences as well as host them."

Another one of Velma friends, who had yet to speak until then, spoke up. "Excuse me, but I'm going to head over to the Chanel Shop while you girls talk. Text me when you're ready to move on." She eyed Esther. "I don't have time to spare on what used-to-be. Now is what's important." She tossed a business card at Esther as she passed by as if she couldn't be bothered with her.

Out of politeness, Esther reached out and grabbed it, even though the woman had been incredibly rude. She couldn't find words to describe what had just happened. *What was that about?* She glanced down at the card.

Bock & Associates Event Planning, LLC

"I like to encourage women, but sometimes that means reminding them that if they plan to get anywhere, they'll have to remove the stick up their behind." Velma shook her head in amusement, and they both laughed. "I apologize, that was my friend Deborah. Esther, tell me, do you live around here? I saw you looking at the red dress in the storefront. That's one seriously hot dress!"

Esther's enthusiasm over the dress had subsided during the perplexing conversation, but Velma picked it up and held it out to Esther. "You should try it on!"

"Well, actually, I never celebrated my birthday and was planning to do so. I thought a new dress for the occasion might be in order."

"Wow, really? We should go together and travel to an Island or something like that. I know you're not celebrating your 50th in a bar! You need to live a little!"

"I don't… I was only going to invite a few ladies, no big ordeal. Fifty is something I want to get beyond; if I don't hurry, I'll be celebrating Fifty-one before I have time to blink."

"When the last time you went to a party and just had fun? Hey, from what I remember from high school, you were always afraid to step out and experience life. Relax and live!"

"You're right, 'use to' being the operative phrase. I'm not that person anymore. I've come a long way. I'm not afraid anymore. I'm evolving."

"Hey, one thing I've learned is that change happens with or without you. When was the last time you actually took a look in the mirror? We all change over time—life forces you to—we get older, we gain wrinkles, we gain weight, and even years of personal baggage… but some change you have to make for yourself—it's a conscious decision—and that is the most important change of all."

Esther was tired of listening to Velma. She wasn't telling Esther anything she didn't already know but was repeating it like it was an original idea. She wasn't listening to what Esther had to say. She wished she could start her day over again, and avoid the whole conversation.

Over Velma's shoulder, Esther noticed that three other women waited outside, and Deborah had already returned. Esther decided to avoid everyone by going into the dressing room to try on the dress she so admired. Hell, the day had already been hectic. Between Vashti's accident, the man on the A Train, and Valerie's confession, she was at the end of her tolerance for the day. She couldn't even begin to imagine if all Velma's friends were like the obnoxious Deborah.

She took the dress from Velma, made her excuses, and made her way to the dressing room, where she remained as she gathering her thoughts. Before long, she closed her eyes and fell asleep.

Esther Arrested

There were six dressing rooms in the Boutique called: *Wo**Men** on **Notice** Boutique*. The store had four sales associates, but no one bothered to check the dressing rooms before closing.

Esther awakened several hours after the boutique had closed and found herself sitting in the dark, clutching the red dress. She panicked and began banging on the wall.

The alarm sounded.

"God, what happened?" She screamed into the dark and fumbled for her phone. She immediately dialed 911.

"Nine-One-One, what's your emergency?"

The 911 operator's voice came in clear and monotone over the line.

"Help! I fell asleep in the dressing room and now the burglar alarm is going off. I can't believe no one checked the dressing rooms before they closed! I don't know why the alarm is going off—I swear I'm not a burglar!

"Ma'am, please calm down and speak slowly—what is your emergency, and where are you?"

"My name is Esther, and I'm locked in the Women on Notice Boutique. I fell asleep in the dressing room. The store is closed, and now the alarm is going off."

"You're in the Women on Notice Boutique that's at Fifth Avenue and Broadway?"

"Yes!"

"Okay, Esther. I need you to get down on the floor and lay there until the officers come. Do not move and I'll communicate the unusual circumstances to the NYPD in your vicinity, I'll also alert the business owner and the alarm company."

Esther hit the floor with her hands raised, unsure if she was going to make it out alive. As she lay face down, she could see flashing lights reflecting off the walls of the dressing room from the picture window at the front of the store. There were voices outside.

She wanted to get up but recalled the operator telling her not to move. Esther began to shake as she heard keys and a lock turn. Two officers entered, guns drawn, and called out for her to stay on the floor and keep her hands raised.

"Please, don't shoot!" She followed their instructions. "I fell asleep, I didn't break in!"

The officer handcuffed Esther and asked her to be quiet and stand on her feet. As she started to speak, the officer raised his voice and said, Ma'am, stand. She struggled on one knee at a time until fully facing the officer. She was completely in a daze.

"What is your name?" One of the officers asked.

"Esther." She nervously chuckled.

"Do you have any identification?"

"Yes, in my purse."

"Ma'am, why are you in the store at 1 AM? The store clearly closes at 7 PM." He asked the other officer rummaged in her purse for her ID.

"I fell asleep in the dressing room—that's all. I didn't know the store had closed, and I guess none of the employees checked out the dressing rooms before they locked up for the night." After a few minutes, and after finding no forced entry, the store owners were lead into the boutique. Unfortunately, Esther didn't recognize them. Neither one had been present in the store when she'd entered earlier in the day.

"Ma'am, I'm sorry, but we have to take you to the station. You'll appear before a judge in the morning." The second officer said.

"Excuse me? I don't understand. I only fell asleep. Officer, why are you taking me to jail?" Esther asked.

The officer didn't answer her questions, but instead, read Esther her Miranda Rights and then walked Esther out of the boutique in handcuffs to his squad car. People stood in the street watching the commotion, and a reporter stood off to one side, their back to the squad car as they gave a news report amidst bright lights and a small camera crew. As the camera turned her way, Esther put her head down, attempting to hide her face.

The Squad Car

What the hell just happened? She had only fallen asleep in the boutique. It wasn't as if she'd robbed the place. It was the employee's negligence that had stranded her in the boutique—surely the officers must understand that. How had she ended up in the back of a squad car? Was she really being arrested?

"Officer, why are you taking me to jail? Do I really look like a burglar to you?" Esther asked again.

"Ma'am, calm down."

"I *am* calm. I'm only asking a simple question."

"Look, I don't really care what you look like, and before you start in on telling me your sob story, I really don't give a f**k. All right? Everyone has their own problems, even me."

"But I—"

"Every day I leave home fearful of not returning, and if I decided who was innocent of a crime based solely on what they looked like, a lot more innocent people would be in jail." The officer glanced back at

Esther in the rearview mirror. "I was married for five years. Now I'm divorced with a 4-year-old son, little Markey. I was on desk duty when I received a call from my ex that our son wasn't responding like he normally would, and he was disoriented. When I met my ex-wife at the hospital they found he had lost a lot of blood and needed a transfusion."

"I'm sorry to hear that."

"What do you think happened when I tried to donate my blood for his transfusion? Hm?"

"Well, I'd hope that your son was okay—"

Officer Mark swerved abruptly and pulled over to the side of the street. He banged heavily on the dashboard with his fists in what appeared to be a nervous breakdown. The man had snapped. He shoved open his door, and got out, pacing around the vehicle about three times and holding his head as if it were about to explode. Then, he angrily climbed back into the driver's seat, slamming the door closed.

Esther stared on in silence, her mouth open in shock.

Officer Mark was a big guy. Easily 5'9 and 240 lbs, with huge hands and small feet for his body. Here Esther sat, handcuffed in the back of a squad car, with an emotionally unstable man who currently in charge of her freedom and safety.

"Lord, Lord, Lord." She must've said it under her breath a hundred times. At this point she wanted to run. Because of the handcuffs she stayed. She did the only thing she could do and began to pray.

"He's not my f**king son! My wife cheated on me, probably for years!" Officer Mark shouted, startling Esther out of her prayers momentarily.

Lord have Mercy on this man's life. Take these stresses and messes away from him quickly, and while you're at it, Lord, get me the hell out of here. Amen.

Esther's one comfort was the knowledge that officer Mark's camera was recording. The area was known to be high trafficked and under heavy surveillance, with street cams along the entire street. The neighborhood was a popular hot spot because of a nightclub called: Gi Gi's Dance-All-Night Club that sat just across the street from where they were parked.

Esther nervously sat waiting. She stared at the sign for Gi Gi's, afraid to speak lest she aggravate Officer Mark any further. After a few tense moments, punctuated by the erratic thumping of Officer Mark's fist against the steering wheel, another squad car approached, it's headlights lighting up the interior of their car.

The officers from the other car jumped from their car, perhaps having sensed that something was wrong, or having seen the movement of their parked car as Office Mark thumped angrily against the interior. They snatched open the driver side door, grabbing Officer Mark to remove him from the car.

A third officer that Esther didn't know held Mark away from the car, his arms trapped behind him in a body hold. After a few seconds of struggle, and then placating rocking, the other officers were able to mollify him. A fourth officer approached, shouting at Officer Mark, "Mark, I don't want to taze you, calm the f**k down!"

"You need to take a leave of absence, man. You can't be breaking down on the job like this." The officer holding onto Officer Mark added, his arms still locked around him.

Up until now, Esther had stayed quiet in the back seat, but It'd been hours since she'd last used a restroom. Eager to get out of the squad car, she leaned back in the seat and began kicking the door to get the other Officer's attention.

"Hey!" She kicked at the door again, grabbing the attention of the Officers, and the one that had threatened to taze Officer Mark jogged over to the squad car, jerking open the door.

"Are you all right, Ma'am?"

"No, I'm not all right. I need to use a restroom."

Man in Blue

The officer immediately apologized to Esther and after making a few hurried remarks to his fellow officers escorted her inside Gi Gi's. He removed her cuffs and waited outside of the restroom door.

Gi Gi's had a lavishly decorated lounge area in the restroom. Esther was drawn in by the inviting atmosphere and decided to sit and collect herself until the officer called for her. The lounge seat was a vast improvement over the backseat of the squad car out front. A bang on the door alerted Esther to the presence of a young woman who entered the restroom.

"Uh, Ma'am? The officer outside asked me to tell you to wash up while you're here, he'll be letting you go." The woman delivered her message and then disappeared into a stall further into the restroom.

"Thank you!" Esther called after her. She stood and looked into the mirror over the row of sinks. She seemed to have aged 10 years in the last few hours. Embarrassed, she grabbed a handful of paper towels and removed the mascara that had smudged terribly.

Her purse had been confiscated at the boutique, so her faded lipstick couldn't be repaired. The only thing Esther wanted to do was to get back home.

Esther exited the restroom to find the officer standing idly against the wall outside. He was easy on the eye, she noted for the first time.

He stood away from the wall as he noticed her, and stuck out his hand. "All set? I'm sorry I didn't introduce myself earlier. Jeff Boyd."

"Jeff… I'm Esther. Are you f**king kidding me? "Ma'am—"

"I've been sitting in the back of a squad car while Mark, your fellow officer, went Rambo. Am I still under arrest? Because the only thing I've done is fall asleep in a dressing room. It wasn't intentional—I didn't steal anything. I don't really understand why I can't just go home. I've been gone since yesterday and I really need to get back across the bridge to Jersey City, get in my car, and drive the hell off into the Grand Canyon. This has been the worst twenty-four hours ."

Jeff, stood casually with one hand rested on the side of his holster and the other on his handcuffs. Although the lady in the restroom had said the officer was going to free her, Esther didn't see how that could be the case. She turned around with her back to him, her hands behind her. "Do it. Cuff me, and let's get this over with."

"You hungry?"

"What? Are all you officers crazy?"

"No. Look, I understand the ordeal you were in with my buddy and I want to make things right. So, instead of booking you at the station, I'm going to let you go. My shift is over in about thirty minutes and I'll be glad to take you home, or back to your car."

Esther could only stare at the officer in surprise.

"It was Mark that wanted to book you—it was his call, and I don't think it was the right one. There was no evidence to convict you on. 911 clocked your call several seconds after the alarm, and a few witnesses called in and said you were in the store earlier in the day."

"Wait, how did they know?"

Jeff smiled a genuine, warm expression. "You were on the news."

"Oh," was all she could think of to say. She was embarrassed, angry, and emotionally exhausted from the events of the last few days. She wanted to scream and cry and hit something. So she did. She started beating on the officer's chest with her clenched fists, laying part of the blame, perhaps unfairly, on him.

"Hey—hey!" He grabbed both of her arms and held them until she calmed down.

They stared at one another for a long time, evaluating each other. *He really is handsome.*

For a moment they both forgot Jeff was still on duty, and Esther had only just narrowly escaped spending the night in lock-up. Esther eased toward him, wanting to be caressed by the warm, rough hands that held her arms firmly between them.

Something changed in Jeff's eyes, a spark of interest, but he let her go and stepped back. "Let me escort you."

They left Gi Gi's and drove to the precinct where Jeff told Esther to stay in the lobby until he had her personal things released from evidence. Within fifteen minutes Jeff was off duty and held her purse in his hands as he collected her and ushered her outside. They climbed into Jeff's red Ford Mustang and drove away, headed towards the George Washington Bridge.

Do you want to get something to eat before I take you back home?" Jeff asked after a few minutes of driving.

"I'm funky. I need to shower and get some rest. I have a friend hospitalized and I need to go see her." Esther declined his offer, glancing out the window.

"What happened?"

"The accident a week ago on the George Washinton Bridge. One of the cars belonged to my friend."

"The yellow sports car? I was on-scene. Bad wreck. How is your friend? Two people were injured; the driver had minor injuries, and the passenger suffered severe injuries. From the report, the woman wasn't in her seat belt."

Esther nodded. "The woman, Vashti, is my friend."

"The guy, his name was Paul, right? Lucky son-of-a-gun."

According to the officer that had written the report, there had been some hanky panky going on. The passenger in the car wasn't wearing a seatbelt. The driver had closed his eyes out of ecstasy and had not noticed the bridge had started to back up. He'd opened his eyes again to see the back of a delivery truck that had jackknifed them, dragging the car across the bridge.

"So that's Paul…"

Jeff looked over at her, a question in his gaze.

"Sorry, I didn't know who was with her, but she kept calling for a Paul in the hospital. Do you know what happened to him?"

"Well, your friend was air-lifted to a nearby hospital, and I believe Paul was taken to another hospital—he was less critical. Tell me, where are you parked? Are you sure you don't want to grab a bite to eat?"

"Make a right at the corner, my car should be there."

Jeff pulled into the lot next to Esther's car, she smiled politely and took a deep breath. "Thank you."

"Here." Jeff handed her his number. "In case you want to grab that dinner sometime, or if you need to talk."

Tired and frustrated, a few minutes later Esther peeled out of the parking lot. She drove for about ten minutes when she looked in her rearview mirror and noticed Jeff, following her. She hadn't thought he'd been serious about escorting her home. Why would he?

Maybe I should have taken him up on that dinner invite. Though I'd much rather take him home...

She stuck her hand out the window and waved to let him know she saw him following her. When Esther arrived home, she waved for Jeff to park and come on in. She needed to relieve her frustration and hoped Jeff would be up for it. Esther pulled into her driveway and Jeff parked out front on the street.

Officer Jeff Boyd

After parking, Esther unlocked her front door and Jeff followed close behind her. Esther started walking towards the kitchen when suddenly he grabbed her.

"Hey, hold on!" Esther shouted out of surprise.

"Come on, you know you women like it rough." Before Esther could respond, Jeff picked her up, pushing her head forward. He tore through her clothes and penetrated her from behind.

"Stop! You're hurting me—stop it!" Esther fought and yelled out of fear.

He clamped his hand over her mouth. "Shut the f**k up." His voice held a gravely, deep tone that seemed to echo in the otherwise silent house.

Esther whimpered as he was too aggressive with her. He grunted like an animal as he pushed into her as if he was pushing through a brick wall. He grabbed his handcuffs and cuffed her hands behind her back at an awkward, hurtful angle. Her voice was weak from fear and pain as she tried to protest.

"Please, you're hurting me!"

"Whore, this is what you wanted. I saw how you looked at me at Gi Gi's, so don't waste my f**king time, bi**h." His grunts morphed into a sound like a bull clearing its throat; loud and vibrational.

He turned Esther over and carried her to the bed, laying her on her back as he climbed on top of her. He unbuttoned his shirt and her blouse, nearly popping the buttons off. He squeezed her breast, hard.

"Jeff, please stop," Esther begged, trying to wiggle out from under him—but he didn't stop.

He slapped Esther, dazing her, then took his penis in his hand. "Make me come bi**h."

"No. stop!" Esther cried out.

He crawled up her body until his knees were at her ears and his penis lay heavily on her face. He took his right arm and grabbed Esther's legs, pulling them up into a position where he could take his hand and penetrate her.

"Jeff, please stop!" She continued to plead, but he shoved his penis into her mouth, effectively silencing her cries.

"Bi**h make me come and shut up."

Esther gagged and turning her head until his penis released. "I'm going to report you! I said no, and you're forcing yourself on me. Stop!"

Her threats went unheeded. He flipped her up, almost onto her head, and had his way with her until he came, regardless of what she said or how hard she struggled to get out from under him.

Afterward, she inched away from him like a caterpillar on its side, her hands still cuffed behind her. "Why are you doing this?"

Jeff got up, pulled on his shirt, and began to rebutton it. He'd never removed his pants during the entire event, and the friction from the fabric had rubbed Esther raw.

"Get these cuffs off me and get the hell out my house!"

Jeff stood there, staring at her with a smirk on his face. "Tell me, was that the way you like it? You women don't want a man to respect you. You only want a big d**k, a good f**k, and money. Which would you have preferred, to be with that crazy a** Mark, sit in a jail cell, or me f**king you? Those were your choices. Did you think I was going to let you off easy? You could have asked me to take you to the precinct and book you. Admit, this was much better than being booked and sitting on a hard bench. A hard d**k is better."

"Please leave." Esther's phone rang, and she struggled to reach it, managing to land on the floor beside the bed, but Jeff moved it away from her.

"They can wait." He grabbed Esther again while she laid on the floor and spread her legs. "You're still under arrest, and no phone calls are allowed in my cell."

At this point, Esther knew she'd have to play the game to survive. He was just as crazy as Officer Mark, a maniac!

She opened her legs wide and looked up at him. "You're small talk and all mouth."

He paused. "What do you mean, that I have a small d**k?"

"Turn me over and remove the cuffs and I'll do more than just lay here like a limp rag."

He seemed to think it over for a moment, and then he reached and grabbed the keys from behind him. He turned her back onto her stomach, still penetrating her from behind, and removed her cuffs. Esther's wrists were near raw from all the friction. She could barely move her arms, as they'd been behind her for a while.

Once the cuffs were removed she began to kick.

Esther screamed harder, she wasn't feeling anything but the adrenaline and she slapped him hard across the face.

"Hit harder." He grunted, seeming to enjoy the pain.

Esther balled her fist and socked him in the jaw as hard as she could. He seemed stunned by the sudden pain in his jaw and she scrambled away from him, grabbing her phone and sprinting towards the bathroom. She locked the door behind her as quickly as she could. "God, help me—I'm calling 911!" She shouted through the door. *Lord, what should I do?*

Jeff was insane and seemed to have become enraged. He shouted and banged on the door in a fit of fury, and then went silent.

Esther sat on the edge of the bathtub and waited in the silence. The house was quiet and she didn't know if Jeff had left or if he still waited on the other side of the door. She didn't know if she should call 911—would they even believe her word against his? She called Elizabeth instead.

"Hello? Esther, we've been calling you. How's everything?"

Esther sniffled. "Please come over with Rachel. Something terrible has happened. I'm scared." Even she could hear the distress in her voice.

"We'll be there shortly. Will you be safe until then?"

She glanced to the locked door. "For now. Hurry."

A few minutes later, Esther's phone rang. "Hello?"

"We're here. Is it safe to come in?" Elizabeth asked.

"Is there a red Mustang parked at the curb?"

"Yes."

"Write down the plates. He—he raped me!"

"Oh my God-" Esther heard Elizabeth mumbled on the other end of the phone as she snapped a picture of the Mustang's plates. "Got it—he's coming out!"

"Don't let him see you!" Esther cried into the phone.

There was silence on the other end of the phone as Jeff pulled away.

"I got a shot of his plates and his face as he drove off. Your house address is in the background." Rachel said, having grabbed the phone out of Elizabeth's hand. "We're coming in."

Rachel immediately uploaded the pictures to her dropbox account, emailed a set to Elizabeth and Esther, making sure the evidence couldn't get lost. She also uploaded and ordered copies at a nearby Walgreens in the area.

No Meant No

Elizabeth and Rachel stared at each other as they exited the car, not knowing what to expect. They slowly approached the front porch, only wanting to see Esther as they always had. Sweet, concerned, and eager to change her life for the better. The last time they'd parted she was on a celebratory journey to plan her past 50th birthday.

Rachel gently knocked on the door, and Esther appeared, dazed, a few long minutes later. All three women stood there in silence, it was as though Esther didn't know whether to let them in or not.

Elizabeth opened the door for her and walked in.

The women were silent as they looked around the house and saw things were out of order. Esther looked liked a used rag doll that had been restuffed the wrong way.

"Esther your wrist. Rachel, take a picture." Elizabeth ordered, noticing the red marks and bruises on her skin.

"No! don't do it. It was my fault. All my fault. I told him to come in after he followed me. I wanted to relieve my frustrations. I wanted to get home. Why didn't he stop?" Esther scrambled through her explanation of the events, but it was all jammed together in her panic.

"Wait, was this a cop? Someone you trusted to uphold the law, someone you go to when someone breaks the Law? This one fool gives a bad name to the men in blue who want justice for victims."

"Yes! That's why I trusted him—I didn't think he could do something like this." Esther nodded, hugging herself.

"Do you understand there could be more women like yourself? Don't let this bastard get away with it. We need to file a report." Elizabeth encouraged her.

Elizabeth and Rachel both stood and grabbed Esther and cried as they hugged her, knowing what needed to be done. They felt Esther pain in silence; there were very few words to be said.

Rachel found a coat for Esther, grabbed her purse, and shoes. She brushed her hair back from her face.

"No meant no. They're not going to treat us women like we don't belong, or like we're ragdolls to be used and then thrown away." Elizabeth angrily complained. She paced back and forth, while Esther remained silent. They knew she would talk when the time came. "Esther, Esther, Esther, we will win. We will stand together and fight!"

The women left and proceeded to a nearby hospital to file rape charges against Officer Jeff Boyd. After that, they planned to go directly to the New York City Police Department -13th Precinct.

At the emergency entrance, a security guard asked them if a wheelchair was needed. At the same time, the ladies all replied. "Yes!"

It was a tense moment as Esther registered, while Rachel and Elizabeth sat in the waiting area. There were several people waiting. While Elizabeth was looking through a magazine, the news flashed about a Manhattan boutique had been burglarized and the female suspect had been apprehended. There looking into the camera was Esther's face.

Elizabeth's whole body clenched as Rachel grabbed her arm, they seemed to be frozen in time.

"What the hell did I just watch?" Elizabeth nearly shouted. "Esther. Not our Esther? Something is wrong."

They immediately went to registration, but Esther had already been taken back. Rape victims it seemed, were taken back to collect as much evidence as quickly as possible.

Esther laid in a cold room with her feet in stirrups, waiting to have a rape kit completed.

More than an hour had passed when Rachel went to the front to question about Esther. They were told the hospital had documented everything and that they were waiting for the officers to come and take her report.

"Can I get a copy of your document?" Elizabeth asked.

"No, sorry. We can't give out patient information to anyone but immediate family members, next of kin, or someone she's already designated to receive a copy of her records."

"Please check her authorization form for my name." Elizabeth knew Esther was an only child, her parents were deceased and they were the only ones close to Esther. She gave her full name to the nurse.

"Ah, yes, there's a Rachel Max and Elizabeth Carter listed." The nurse checked their ID's, and then asked them to follow her. They passed the area Esther was in, and they could see her talking to two police officers. From the back, it appeared one was a male and the other was a female.

The nurse explained that there was evidence of forced entry to Esther's body. She had torn tissues that were evident of someone who'd suffered abuse against their will. "We'll be given her some sedatives and may keep her a couple days for observation, she's showing signs of shock. Sometimes after a rape, victims may become suicidal or depressed, she explained. "As her friends, she'll need your support. She may want to talk about it, she may not. Try to have patience and understanding."

"We will." The two women agreed. In the room they were in, another news alert flashed about the Manhattan Boutique Burglary and Elizabeth tried to divert the nurse's attention away from the television. She did not want her to pass judgment on Esther. "I'm sorry I didn't ask before. What is your name? I'm Elizabeth." "Julie." The nurse shook her hand. "Please keep this off the records, but your friend will win as long as she doesn't give up. Here's my card, my cell number, and may I have yours? I've had patients I've sympathized with before, but out of all my years working as a nurse, I've never gone into the bathroom and cried mid-shift. Your friend is devasted. Apparently, she must have known the guy who did this to her?"

"You don't know? It was a cop! She didn't know him really, but she felt comfortable because he represented the law." Elizabeth explained.

"What precinct?"

"New York, 13th precinct."

"Wow, that's a relief, different state and county. It was smart to take her to another precinct's jurisdiction."

Nurse Julie advised them to go back to the waiting area and explained that when everything was checked out she'd call them to go back to see their friend.

Rachel was glad that the nurse was nice and seemed to understand the pain and hurt Esther had suffered.

Elizabeth understood going up against the men in blue could sometimes be difficult. She tried not to worry about it. The truth was there—they had evidence. She knew once the news hit the airwaves, lawyers were going to come out of the sky looking to defend such a high-profile case. She only hoped the right one for Esther would fall right into her lap. *God, we're trusting you for this one.*

"One of the good things about this is, she'll live through it. She survived." Rachel said as she and Elizabeth held hands in support of their friend.

After awhile, nurse Julie called for them to come back. Rachel and Elizabeth joined their friend.

Esther reached out to them for a hug. "I can't believe I've made it this far. I know the road ahead of me may be long, but with God and friends like you guys, I'll make it through. I'm going to make that bastard pay."

Esther didn't understand why God had let the last twenty-four hours she had experienced happen. She knew there was a lesson in everything, though and God still reigned in her life. He was her strength and she needed to keep going. Esther dozed off while talking to Elizabeth and Rachel.

Room #1833

Nurse Julie confirmed that Esther would be in the hospital for a couple days, in room 3318 in South Tower, and gave Elizabeth Esther's personal belongings. She advised them to let her rest, and that the medication she was on would have her out for most of the day and night. She told them they could check with the head nurse on the floor she'd be on. She told them goodbye, and both women thanked Julie for her help.

As they were leaving the hospital, Esther's cell phone rang in her purse. Elizabeth didn't know if she should answer until she noticed the caller ID—the number was from the hospital. Concerned that it might be nurse Julie calling, Elizabeth answered. "Hello?" "Hello, this is Vashti's nurse. I'm calling to inform you that she's alert and progressing and able to receive visitors."

"Thank you. This is Esther's friend. Esther is currently here in the hospital also in room #3318 South. What is the room number for Vashti?"

"Vashti is in the North ICU unit room #1833. She'll be glad to have company. She's had no visitors so far. When you come to the floor press the red button to be let in."

After the nurse hung up, Elizabeth and Rachel stood and shook their heads.

"Can you believe they're both in the hospital, in different towers?" Elizabeth mused.

They were both really tired and had never met Vashti. They debated if they should visit or not. After thinking about Esther, unable to visit Vashti, they decided to meet Vashti, because Esther would've wanted to check on her friend.

Elizabeth Meets Vashti

After reaching the North ICU unit, they were buzzed in and were directed to room #1833. When they walked in the room, Vashti was sitting up, bandaged in a head wrap, and her bruises were still visible. Vashti stared at Elizabeth and Rachel.

"Do I know you? You may have the wrong room."

"Hello, my name is Rachel. We're friends of Esther," Rachel spoke up.

"I'm Elizabeth." Elizabeth waved.

Vashti broke down crying. She must've cried for twenty minutes while Elizabeth and Rachel looked on in awkward silence, unsure of what to do.

"What's wrong, Vashti? We didn't mean to upset you, did we say anything wrong?" Rachel asked.

"Where's Esther? Has anyone seen Paul?"

Elizabeth started thinking back to how long it had been since she and Paul had broken up. Was Vashti's Paul her ex? "Excuse me, did you say Paul? Do you have a picture of him? Do you know how we can contact him for you? Is there someone we can call for you?"

Rachel did a triple spin and silently counted backward from ten. Meanwhile, Elizabeth patiently waited for Vashti to reply.

"Yes, here's his picture. He was in the accident with me. I have not heard from him since I've been hospitalized. I don't know if he's alive or... Have you heard anything on the news about the accident?"

The picture confirmed that Paul was Elizabeth's ex.

"Vashti, me meeting you, is in divine order. I've also asked, 'where's Paul'. I'm Paul's ex-wife. He walked out and I haven't seen him for at least two years. I believe that may be about the time you two met. He loves young and pretty... and I'm sorry to say, right now, that you're not. Brace yourself for what I'm about to tell you: Paul, is not coming back. I know that's not what you want to hear, but it's probably best if you move on and find a way to heal instead. I will never mention his name again to you, nor should you to me. I came in peace and I'm leaving in peace."

Vashti's was still connected to a monitor and it began beeping and buzzing loudly in response to her stress. The ICU nurses on the floor ran into the room, asking the two women to leave as they began to resuscitate her. Elizabeth and Rachel hadn't noticed that Vashti had actually passed out in the chaos.

On the elevator, Rachel turned to Elizabeth. "Wow! I would never have imagined you meeting that woman like this."

Esther had known the whole time.

"Knowing Esther, she probably knew it was just a matter of time. I respect that. I've been freed. No more pole-jumping for me. That was the key my soul yearned for to let him go, and now I can. Eventually, all secrets come to the light. I guess God was holding on to that one until I was ready to heal, and I am. Thank God I've been set free."

Red Mustang

Elizabeth and Rachel smiled as they traveled back to take Rachel to her car, which they'd left at Esther's house. They pulled up and noticed from afar there was a Red Mustang parked in front of Esther's house again.

"Oh my…" sighed Elizabeth.

"That bastard has come back. What do we do?" Rachel asked.

Together, they came up with a plan. They'd park away from him and joyfully walk up to the door and knock to see if he'd acknowledge them. Elizabeth parked her car and they proceeded as planned. Before they could get on the porch, the door of the red Mustang flew open and out jumped Officer Jeff Boyd.

"Hold it right there, I'm Officer Boyd, and I'm looking for burglar suspect Esther Cox. Do you know where she might be?" He demanded.

Elizabeth and Rachel were both shocked at the aggressiveness of his tone and words. It was obvious he was mentally disjointed. He stood with his hand resting on his holster and there was something very strange about his eyes. There was violence in his eyes, as though he wasn't quite human anymore—he reminded them of a demon. They knew they had to answer very carefully.

"Officer, I do recall seeing the news. Did this person escape custody? Have you seen or heard the latest news? I believe the woman you're looking for has been captured. When the last time you checked with the 13th Precinct?" Elizabeth asked. She hoped the questions she raised would get him to rethink the situation. Officer Jeff stood motionless for a short period, then turned around like a robot.

They watched him as he drove away until he reached the corner. Elizabeth and Rachel sat down on the porch steps.

"What was that all about?" Rachel knew they had to move quickly, Esther would be released from the hospital in a few days, and her home may not be safe for her.

Elizabeth noticed the accumulated mail in her mailbox. There were several letters from law firms. She grabbed them, and they both drove away in their separate cars.

Rachel Meets Valerie

Rachel continued on to Walgreens to get copies of the pictures she'd ordered. On entry into Walgreen's her phone rang. It was Valerie.

"Hello?" she answered her phone.

"Hi, have you talked to Esther? I wanted to let her know that John passed today. I wasn't sure if she'd heard or not."

"Oh, my! Well right now is not the time to tell her. Can you meet me on the nature trail in twenty minutes?"

"Sure," Valerie agreed.

Rachel picked up the pictures and proceeded to meet with Valerie. From what Rachel understood about Valerie, she chose not to watch the news stations on television or listen to them on the radio. It was her way of blocking out negativity in order to remain positive. Rachel arrived and found Valerie was there waiting. She approached her with a hug like no other. Valerie knew from her approach that something was definitely going on.

"Is everything okay, your hug was very intense," Valerie asked.

"It's Esther. The news is saying she burglarized a store, but it's not true—and she was raped by one of the police officers. She's been hospitalized."

Valerie fell to the ground in shock and grabbed her head as she held it down between her knees. Rachel joined her in support, holding onto Valerie for support.

"Everything's going to work out," Rachel assured her, "Esther agreed to file charges against the NYPD."

"You've got to be joking! This is serious... it was only two weeks ago that we visited Vashti in the hospital together."

"We visited Vashti and introduced ourselves, Elizabeth and I." I'll let her share that with you. For now, we need to help Esther and bring her back to her natural self. We have work to do. As a matter of fact, I have several letters that were mailed to her from lawyers. I'll drop them off. Come on, let's go and visit our friend. You can hop in the car with me, and I'll bring you back. She needs to decide who will represent her, and I'm not sure if she has or not.

Valerie and Rachel proceeded to the hospital to visit with Esther.

Room #3318

Upon arrival, they found Elizabeth was already there. Esther looked good given her situation. Her energy level was coming back, even though her nurse requested they keep their visit with her short. The women paid her little mind—this was their friend.

Esther and Elizabeth both acknowledged Valerie and Rachel. Rachel was deciding if she should show the pictures she'd picked up from Walgreen's and figured it was not the right time. So, instead, she remembered to give Esther, the mail she'd taken from her box.

Esther was delighted they'd taken the mail from her box. Rachel didn't mention when they'd returned that officer Jeff Boyd was there.

"Did I mention, that bastard said he was coming back? Do you believe he would come back and do what he did over and over again?" Esther began to get upset just thinking about it.

Valerie held her hand. "Esther, everytime you think of him. Just remember that you're doing something to prevent him from ever coming back again. We are very proud of your courage for taking the steps to stop him. He's threatening you because he wants to dissuade you from filing charges. It won't work. We won't let it."

Rachel spoke up. "Take some time to choose your attorney. We're going to come back later. Get some rest, okay?"

Elizabeth and Valerie nodded their encouragement. Everyone turned to walk away.

"Valerie, have you heard anything about John?" Esther asked, delaying their exit.

"Yes. I'm sorry Esther, he passed earlier this morning," Valerie replied.

Esther nodded, accepting this news, and one tear fell. She grabbed the letters they'd left for her and slid down under the covers as everyone vacated the room.

"Wow! John, passed," Elizabeth spoke as they left the hospital. "I was hoping one day to meet him. Oh well, I need a massage. My back feels like a dry, tight desert. Anyone for a spa day?" She glanced around to gage the other women's reactions. "You know what? Nevermind. Retract what I said. I can't sit still long enough. Oh! I just remembered. I have Esther's phone. I'll take it back and I'll catch up with you girls later."

The other women said their goodbyes to Elizabeth. She returned to Esther's room and found Esther sitting up, looking at the mail she'd received.

"That was quick."

"I returned to give you your personal things and your phone. Also, I wanted to let you know that I met Vashti. She's doing well and she knows about Paul and me." Esther raised her eyebrows.

"I'll tell you about it later. That's not really why I returned—I wanted to let you know that Vashti is alert. The nurse called to update you, and I answered your phone."

"Thanks for letting me know. Oh, I was thinking about using female Attorney Alexandra Alex… but I read this one letter from Attorney Abraham Joseph. What do you think?" Esther handed the letter to Elizabeth.

> *Dear Esther Cox,*
>
> *You have the right to be respected for saying no! No one is above the Law. You must stand for your rights and fight for justice, and the rights of all mankind to be protected. It only takes one person that's willing to rise up! I'm hoping that person is you. I will stand with you and fight for your rights.*
>
> *I may not get back what has been taken away from you, however, you'll have the pride and dignity knowing that you fought for your rights, and other's rights, to carry you the rest of your life.*
>
> *Rise up. The law is on your side.*
>
> *Attorney Abraham Joseph*

"Was he there? How does this guy know so much? Call him Esther. You must move fast. It's going to hit the news sooner or later. The paperwork has already begun. Call Attorney Abraham Joseph now, it seems like he's perfect for your situation," Elizabeth encouraged her.

Attorney Abraham Joseph

Esther contacted Attorney Abraham Joseph, who agreed to come to the hospital. He walked in well dressed and clean shaven. With his tall, lean build, he didn't look like he was the kind to work out. His thin frame seemed a product of the stress of his job. The attorney extended his hands to shake hers.

"I've called a press conference, so be ready—but don't worry. I'll be doing all the talking," he informed her. "Esther, there's no better place to have it than having here in the hospital, given the nature of your assault. There'll probably be some backlash because you were portrayed as someone who broke into a boutique, but we'll do what we can to minimize that. If you can think of anyone that might have witnessed you in the store that day, it would be helpful."

As Esther went through her paperwork she ran across Velma's card. Would Velma stick up for her? They weren't close friends, but she'd definitely witnessed Esther at the boutique and knew she'd gone into the dressing rooms. "I may have a witness."

"Velma, huh? What's the number? I'll give her a call while you freshen up a little for the press conference. I know you women always want to look your best, even when no one expects you to. "

"Will I need to say anything?"

"No, that's why you hired me. The only time you'll talk is when we go to trial. From this moment forward, do not say anything to anyone—and that includes family and friends. No one! The press are like vultures, they'll feed off any scrap they can get ahold of."

"But my friends were the ones that encouraged me to file charges. They kind of already know what happened. Why can't I talk to them about it?"

"I didn't say lose or get rid of your friends. It's just that anything you share with anyone at this point could get out in the wrong way and come back to hurt your case. It's good to have friends. If they're true friends, they wouldn't want to know details, they would understand your need to win."

Esther nodded. She knew he was right—and her friends hadn't asked for details. They'd encouraged her to file charges without prying. They were good friends.

Esther freshened her face and pulled her hair back behind her ears as she prepared for the press conference. The cameramen and Fox News reporters were already coming in to set up for the broadcast.

Meanwhile, the paperwork had started to circulate through the system in the hands of Prosecuting Attorney Faye Howard, who had gone to meet with the Captain and Sargeant of the NYPD 13th Precinct. She was there to advise them that a report had been filed on February 14, 2017, in the 36th District Court alleging that one of their men in blue was being accused of sexually violating a woman in Jersey City. They were still in the process of collecting more data on the matter, but if sufficient evidence was found an arrest warrant would be issued on behalf of the State Of New York. Captain Oscar Goin looked down at the paperwork Faye Howard had brought to him. "Who's the accused?"

"Officer Jeff Boyd." She stated simply, folding her hands in front of her.

"Palmer!"

"Yes, Captain?" The young officer stuck his head inside the Captain's office.

"Any idea where Jeff is?"

"No. No one has an idea where he is or what's going on."

The news was scheduled to hit the airwaves at 12:00 noon. "Da*n."

A small screen in the corner of the Captain's office replayed captions about rape allegations against Officer Boyd, with more details on the 12 o' clock news to come. The whole mess had made the headline news.

North Carolina

Velma's phone rang and she dug it out of her purse to answer it. "Hello?"

"Velma, it's Deb."

"Hey Deb, what's up?"

"I'm coming to your office—we need a meeting."

Velma stared at her phone. Deborah had hung up.

Velma had no idea what Deborah wanted. It must be important for her to drive all the way from the other side of town to hold a meeting. She knew it would take her more than twenty minutes to get there.

She arrived early and waited for Deborah to arrive, unsure why the meeting had been called in the first place.

Finally, Deborah arrived. She walked in and closed Velma's door behind her. With her hands on hips, she scowled at Velma. "What did I say about those high school use to–be's? Maybe you'll listen to me after watching this." She strode towards the TV across the room.

"What the hell is it this time, Deborah? You drove all the way to talk about some high school s**t?"

Deborah popped in a video recording using her Apple TV connection. She wanted to be sure Velma watched it on full screen and not on her iPhone. "Pay attention. Watch!" She paused the recording for

Velma to see that it was Esther on the screen and pointed out the captions. "Recognize her?"

Velma stood tall, both hands on her desk and leaned over and said, "Get the hell out my office."

"Don't get mad at me. I recorded it for you. Why did she break in? We could have purchased a dress, purse, car, shoes and house for her. Choose your friends wisely, please!"

Velma ignored Deborah's gossip. She knew something was not right. Esther didn't need to steal anything. "Do you have any idea who her father is? Google it. Esther can buy several houses and boats for you. Your petty entitlement doesn't belong here. Right now I'm worried about her and I'm trying to figure out what happened. You know I don't trust the NYPD." Velma tapped her fingers on her desk as she thought out loud. "She's going to need a lawyer and support. Burglary? Not Esther. We were there that day--oh my God! I remember her going into the dressing room." She glanced up at the TV screen. "She couldn't have fallen asleep, could she? Oh, Esther. I bet that's what happened. She was probably trying to avoid our crazy a**es after the way you treated her!" She looked at Deborah in disgust. "You need to leave my office—wait. Have a seat."

Deborah laughed, but it didn't hold any genuine amusement. "I can't believe you're trying to figure out how to help that burglar."

"I need to find her number and contact her." Velma hit the intercom button on her office phone. "Cathy?" She addressed her assistant. "I need you to search social media and find everything you can about

Pole-Date Or Soul-Mate

Esther Cox of Jersey City." She couldn't recall getting Esther's number, but she had given Esther her business card. She hoped Esther would call.

"Wait—did I hear you say, Cox? Not Gregg Cox, The philanthropist... the one that owns Cox & Associates Mutual Funds? You, have to be kidding me. She was so humble and simply dressed. She needs to pump it up some, that girl has no idea how to dress."

"Look, Deb, not everyone feels the need to wear their wealth as protective armor. Esther doesn't care about those things. She's never been flamboyant or boastful. Anyone who only cares about money is a da*n fool. Esther is a sweet and humble woman, and she's someone you can trust. I swear you'd drive a fish to swim up Tequila instead of water just to get away from you. Have a good day!"

Embarrassed and angry, Deborah jumped up, grabbed her designer handbag, and strutted out Velma's office in her red bottom heels. She pulled her long flowing hair over her right shoulder and turned to Velma as she left. "Let me know what you find out!"

Velma shook her head. Deborah was her friend, and she loved her, but she knew one day something would knock her off her high horse, and she hoped it was soon.

"Oh my God," Cathy came bursting into her office. "watch the news at twelve. There was a notice on Facebook about a live broadcast." She held out a printed copy of the headlines to Velma.

Woman caught burglarizing an upscale Boutique now accuses officer of NYPD of rape. A press conference will be held @ 12:00 PM EST.

Velma immediately tuned into the local news channel. "Oh no!" She gasped, hoping that it was a different woman and not Esther. What the hell was going on? Her phone rang—Deborah again—but Velma refused to answer.

Woman caught burglarizing an upscale Boutique now accuses officer of NYPD of rape.

The words ran across the bottom of the TV screen.

Press Conference

"I'm Amy Lynn coming to you live from an area hospital in the state of New Jersey. We're here with Attorney Abraham Joseph to learn a little more about the situation." The news reporter began.

Suddenly the screen switched over to focus on a well-dressed man standing before the reporter's microphone. "My client, Esther Cox, has been hospitalized after she was brutally sexually assaulted by an NYPD officer. We cannot comment on the officer's name until evidence and charges are brought forth. On Esther Cox's behalf, I will be seeking criminal and civil damages against The NYPD and the accused officer. We hope that justice will be served for my client. Thank you!"

The reporter reappeared on-screen. "Can you tell us where the assault took place?"

"Questions will be addressed at a later time. My client needs time to rest and heal after her ordeal. We ask that the media please respect that."

Reporter Amy Lynn addressed the viewers, "Well, there you have it. Now keep in mind these are early allegations. The accused officer has not been charged as of yet. Let's replay an earlier video captured with the accused burglar, Esther Cox, being arrested a little over a week ago. Now, I've asked the question, where did the alleged rape take place? That question hasn't been answered at this time. What we do know is that the accuser was in the custody of the NYPD, but no official charges were brought against her. As far as we've been able to discern, Esther Cox was never booked at the 13th Precinct, which begs the question: Where was she taken after this video footage was taken, and how did she end up here at the hospital? We'll update you after more details are gathered. I'm Amy Lynn for Fox 5 News, New York."

Velma stood silent for a minute, staring at the TV screen. She had to do something.

She called her friends and told them to get ready, they were going to New York. She had a friend in need and if they had to, they'd organize a protest!

Cathy stood dumbstruck, aware she'd have to arrange for a flight and hotel room.

Finally, Attorney Abraham Joseph called Velma to schedule a time to speak with her regarding the day she'd run into Esther at The WoMen on Notice Boutique. He wanted to go over what she'd remembered.

"As previously said, I will be representing your friend and she's not being charged with burglary—that's all media hype. Can you recall anything, in particular, that day that stood out? Don't answer now. I want you to think about it and we'll meet at a scheduled time. Do you plan to visit New York soon?" The attorney asked.

"Anything I can do, I will. Esther is not a burglar. I was at the store the day in question along with several of my friends."

"Great! Don't say anything else. I'll be back in contact with you shortly."

"I should be in New York by mid-week, next week. You can find me at the Waldorf Hotel. I'll be in touch." She hung up from the Attorney and then dialed the hospital Esther was in. She figured it had to be nearby in Jersey City where Esther resided. When she called, Elizbeth was there in the room and answered instead of Esther.

"This is Elizabeth, Room 3318. How may I help you?"

"Is this the room of Esther Cox?"

"Why do you ask? May I ask who's calling?"

"To make it short, I'm Velma, an old friend of hers from North Carolina. I will be traveling to New York to support my friend. I've received a call from her attorney, who I plan to meet. While I'm there I was hoping to meet you also."

Elizabeth paused. "Well then, let's exchange numbers. Maybe we can meet once you arrive and settle in. You know, we're in Jersey City and not New York? Esther's resting, but we're hoping she'll be released tomorrow."

"All right, I'll be back in touch shortly." They exchanged numbers, and then Velma called her friends; Deborah, Sabrina, and Shelly. She asked if they were available to take a trip to New York, and they all agreed.

LaGuardia Airport

Later that week, along wth her assistant Cathy, they all boarded a jet from North Carolina, landing at LaGuardia Airport. As they were walking through the Airport to the baggage claim, another Live News alert was broadcast on the airport TV screens.

"I'm Prosecuting Attorney Faye Howard, and on behalf of the NYPD and the State of New York, enough evidence has been gathered in the allegations of sexual assault against accuser Esther Cox. Charges have been filed against Officer Jeff Boyd of the NYPD 13th Precinct. We encourage Mr. Boyd to turn himself in. He has until 5:00 PM today. If you know of Mr. Boyd's whereabouts, we encourage you to contact the NYPD." The attorney nodded to the police Captain to her right.

"On behalf of our fellow officers, we would like to remind everyone that no one is above the law. If my officer is found guilty he shall be prosecuted to the full extent of the law. We will not, and do not, accept this kind of behavior in the NYPD. We will hold a press conference at a later time to address your questions."

"Wow!" Cathy gasped. Everyone jumped up and down and shouted, "Justice for Esther," as they continued to walk through the LaGuardia Airport. Other women that had watched the Live Broadcast throughout the airport joined them chanting all the way to the baggage claim.

Rise up!

"Justice for Esther!" Means "Justice For Us!"

Stay tuned for Volume 3 Coming soon!

- Will Esther win her case?
- Was she at fault?
- Will Vashti bounce back from her accident?
- Will Paul ever resurface?
- Will the women from North Carolina get along with the Jersey women?
- Where did this Lawyer come from?

Express your feedback @Authorantreinastone Facebook page

Join the discussion:
www.theevolvingwomaninyou.com

Book a discussion with the Author:
info@theevolvingwomaninyou.com

Welcome:

Pearls for You Section

Pearls For You

Although it's said that a gentleman lets a woman walk ahead, sit first, and speak first; while he walks on the outside, don't get caught up in the hype. Don't automatically think he's a gentleman because of a one-time nod to chivalry or because he's eager to impress you. Always be in the position to keep your eyes on his hands. Never turn your back to a stranger, and better yet:

"Never trust a man from behind."

So how do you get around it? Simply, walk beside him or behind him. Even when your conversation with another person seems to flatter you and you feel like you can let your guard down, remember that a pole will tell you anything it thinks you want to hear, he only has one thing in mind; how can he penetrate your behind, period.

Many married women and single women are dying for attention. With so many voices in their heads telling them what to do and how to act, it can sometimes cloud their eyes and prevent them from seeing through the fog.

But what if a person is blind?

The instinct of a blind person is much greater than that of a seeing person. They have the ability to detect if something is wrong. They can walk into a room, feel your energy, hear the lies in a person's voice, and detect that something is wrong—because their eyesight can't lie to them.

If we take the time to tune into our surroundings like a blind person and not base everything on what we see, we may understand what we truly feel:

1. We would vacate the relationship we're in.
2. We would've said no, the first time he asked.
3. We would've felt the cold air in the heated bedroom.
4. We would've walked out on stupid when he or she called us stupid.
5. We would know that too much in common could stunt our growth.
6. We would know not to go through their personal things. (Cell phone)
7. We would know that two people can't walk together unless they agree.
8. We would know that man has but one breath in his nostrils.
9. We would know that if you are not growing, you are dying!
10. We would know our purpose is to live and our destiny is death.
11. We would know to love in the moment and not in the B.S. Period.
12. We would know that too many hens (girlfriends) will often leave behind feathers.

13. We would know that we can forgive, but it's hard to remember to forgive.
14. We would know to learn from our experiences and not make the same mistakes.
15. We would be more grateful and not hateful.
16. We would practice being on time and not late.
17. We would know all things work together for the good.
18. We would know to seek wisdom, knowledge, and understanding.
19. We would know the greatest gift of all is LOVE.
20. We would know Love doesn't hurt.

If you don't know Him by now, when will you know?

God, will always be there to hold, Love, protect, give, and feed you. When God attempts to lead us away from a dark path and towards the light, many of us pull away because we are afraid of not knowing or seeing where, what, when, how or why.

You hear people talk about that quiet voice, but how do you connect with it? By opening your Bible and studying the word of God. Can you recognize the Shepherd's voice?

John 10:27 NIV My sheep listen to my voice; I know them, and they follow me.

That voice is whispering to guide you away from hurt and pain, to a place of peace and joy! It is the same voice that rumbles loud like thunder and commands the wind to blow from the south, west, north, and east. It is that voice that every knee shall bow down to and every tongue shall confess.

Romans 14:11 it is written: "'as surely as I live,' says the Lord, 'every knee will bow before me; every tongue will acknowledge God.'"

Proverbs 8:4 NIV "To you, O people, I call out; I raise my voice to all mankind.

When we recognize as men and women that we were created to be a suitable mate for someone; then we'll understand there's someone appropriate for us.

You can make anything work, as long as it's not broken. Don't get your mind and body out of whack, just because the relationship didn't work out. Stand up! Grace saved you. There's something bigger and better coming your way. How will you know if you still look for the same kind of man or woman, love the same way, desire the same things and only gain weight from eating the same foods, and not gaining a heart to desire change by opening your mind, body, and soul to receive more of God's word?

Ephesians 4:15 NIV Instead, speaking the truth in love, we will grow to become in every respect the mature body of him who is the head, that is, Christ.

More importantly, believe that you are different and that special someone is seeking you out. Also, when you begin to know God's word when you are married, you'll understand the man or woman you are married to has the right to move slow to get your request done on their own time. Do not jump up because you want it done right then. If you want to get things done right away, well then, do it yourself. Make it something to remove from your task list.

Seek to understand in every relationship. When you do, you will have peace.

Jeremiah 51:15 NIV "He made the earth by his power; he founded the world by his wisdom and stretched out the heavens by his understanding."

Many people have a big laugh at banged up cars. I recall driving one myself. Maybe you have driven one also. Your friends may have laughed and yet still asked you for a ride. The gas tank was always full; you never had a problem and were able to arrive on time to where you were going. When other late model cars were broke down, God made a way for us to keep going in the so-called pieces of junk. If you're evaluating the outside of a person or thing, take the same time and evaluate the inside. It's not the outside of something that determines if it's junk. The engineering behind everything is on the inside.

Who do you think keeps your engine revved up?

The Ten Virgins

Who took their lamps and went out to meet the bridegroom.
Matthew 25

- Five were wise; they took oil with them in a jar.
- Five were foolish; they didn't take any oil.
- Since the Bridegroom took so long to come, they became tired and fell asleep.
- During the midnight hour, there was a call by The Bridegroom.
- The wise virgins brought extra oil with them so they were prepared.
- The foolish virgins asked the wise virgins to give them some of their oil.
- The wise virgins told them to go to those who sell oil and buy some for themselves.
- While the foolish virgins were gone, the wise virgins were let into the wedding banquet.
- When the foolish virgins returned, knocking on the door to get into the banquet, the Bridegroom opened the door and said: …. I don't know you!

Points Made

- Always be prepared.
- Know your foundation.

- Persevere.
- A champion never gives up. They continue to train and focus on their purpose.
- To live a more abundant life.
- Be prepared for a suitable mate.
- Whom are you going to live for? Then be prepared for the challenge.
- What do you want? Prepare to receive it!

You cannot be a Queen unless you're prepared to go before the King. In the Book of Esther, before she could be considered a candidate to be queen, she had to be prepared by completing twelve months of beauty treatments: six months with oil of myrrh, and six months with perfumes and cosmetics.

Therefore, it's imperative that you always smell, feel and look good. Taking care of your body elevates your mind, and not in an egoist kind of a way. When you take the second, minute, moment or hour you have at hand to pamper yourself, it becomes a habit that you will maintain, even after you connect with a suitable mate. Read Esther 2:12.

God will not rescue you unless you are prepared to be rescued. God will not send you a suitable mate until you are prepared to receive him.

Go before the **King** and receive your **Crown!**

About The Author

Antreina E. Stone writes thought provoking books and speaks to encourage women to turn their thoughts around about men, to analyze their relationships and embrace the love within to build a better relationship with themselves and others. By doing so, a suitable mate will appear and the pole dates disappear, and also for married woman to look at the light and not the things.

Notes

Pole-Date Or Soul-Mate

Antreina E. Stone

www.ingramcontent.com/pod-product-compliance
Lightning Source LLC
Chambersburg PA
CBHW031308060426
42444CB00032B/517